Will Shortz Presents

KENKEN EASY

Volume 2

KenKen™: Logic Puzzles That Make You Smarter!

Will Shortz Presents KenKen Easiest, Volume 1
Will Shortz Presents KenKen Easy, Volume 2
Will Shortz Presents KenKen Easy to Hard, Volume 3
Will Shortz Presents The Little Gift Book of KenKen

KenKen for Kids

Will Shortz Presents I Can KenKen! Volume 1
Will Shortz Presents I Can KenKen! Volume 2
Will Shortz Presents I Can KenKen! Volume 3

WILL SHORTZ PRESENTS

KENKEN EASY

VOLUME 2

100 LOGIC PUZZLES THAT MAKE YOU SMARTER

TETSUYA MIYAMOTO

ST. MARTIN'S GRIFFIN
NEW YORK

WILL SHORTZ PRESENTS KENKEN EASY, VOLUME 2. Puzzle content copyright © 2008 by Gakken Co., Ltd. Introduction © 2008 Will Shortz. All rights reserved. Printed in the United States of America. For information, address St. Martin's Press, 175 Fifth Avenue, New York, N.Y. 10010.

www.stmartins.com

ISBN-13: 978-0-312-38279-7
ISBN-10: 0-312-38279-0

First Edition: October 2008

10 9 8 7 6 5 4 3 2 1

Introduction

If you consider all the world's greatest puzzle varieties, the ones that have inspired crazes over the years—crosswords, jigsaw puzzles, tangrams, sudoku, etc.—they have several properties in common. They . . .

- Are simple to learn
- Have great depth
- Are variable in difficulty, from easy to hard
- Are mentally soothing and pleasing
- Have some unique feature that makes them different from everything else and instantly addictive

By these standards, a new puzzle called KenKen, the subject of the book you're holding, has the potential to become one of the world's greats.

KenKen is Japanese for "square wisdom" or "cleverness squared." The rules are simple: Fill the grid with digits so as not to repeat a digit in any row or column (as in sudoku) and so the digits within each heavily outlined group of boxes combine to make the arithmetic result indicated.

KenKen puzzles start with 3×3 boxes and use only addition. Harder examples have larger grids and more arithmetic operations.

KenKen was invented in 2003 by Tetsuya Miyamoto, a Japanese math instructor, as a means to help his students learn arithmetic and develop logical thinking. Tetsuya's education method is unusual. Put simply, he doesn't teach. His philosophy is to make the tools of learning available to students and then let them progress on their own.

Tetsuya's most popular learning tool has been KenKen, which his students spend hours doing and find more engaging than TV and video games.

It's true that KenKen has great capacity for educating and building the mind. But first and foremost it's a puzzle to be enjoyed. It is to numbers what the crossword puzzle is to words.

So turn the page and begin. . . .

—Will Shortz

How to Solve KenKen

KenKen is a logic puzzle with simple rules:

- Fill the grid with digits so as not to repeat a digit in any row or column.
- Digits within each heavily outlined group of squares, called a cage, must combine to make the arithmetic result indicated.
- A 3×3–square puzzle will use the digits from 1 to 3, a 4×4–square puzzle will use the digits from 1 to 4, etc.

Solving a KenKen puzzle involves pure logic and mathematics. No guesswork is needed. Every puzzle has a unique solution.

In this introductory volume of KenKen, the puzzles use multiplication and division in the following manner:

- In a cage marked with a times sign, the given number will be the product of the digits you enter in the squares.
- In a cage marked with a division sign, the given number will be the quotient of the digits you enter in the squares (the higher digit divided by the lower one).

Take the 5 × 5–square example on this page.

12×		1	2÷	20×
2	15×			
5×	2÷	3	20×	2
		2÷		3÷
20×			3	

To start, fill in the digits in the 1 × 1 sections—the 1 in the top row, the 2 in the second row, etc. This puzzle has five such isolated squares. They are literally no-brainers.

Next, look for sections whose given numbers are either high or low, or that involve distinctive combinations of digits, since these are often the easiest to solve. For example, the top row has a pair of squares with a product of 12. The only two digits from 1 to 5 that multiply to 12 are 3 and 4. We don't know their order yet, but this information can still be useful.

Now look at the pair of squares in the fifth column that have a product of 20. The only two digits from 1 to 5 that multiply to 20 are 4 and 5. The 4 can't go in the top row, because this row already has a 4 (in one of the squares with a product of 12). Therefore, the 5 must go in the top row, and the 4 below it.

Next, look at the pair of squares in the fourth column whose quotient is 2. Among the digits from 1 to 5, two pairs of digits can have a quotient of 2—4 and 2, and 2 and 1. In this case, 4 and 2 aren't the correct pair, since both the first and second rows already have 4s (in the first row, in one of the squares with a product of 12; in the second row, in the fifth column). Therefore, the digits must be 2 and 1. The 1 can't go in the first row, because this row already has a 1. And the 2 can't go in the second row, because this row already has a 2. Thus, the 2 goes in the first row, and the 1 below it.

Sometimes the next step in solving a KenKen puzzle is to ignore the given numbers and use sudoku-like logic to avoid repeating a digit in a row or column. For example, the fifth column in our sample puzzle starts out with 5, 4, and 2. The bottom two squares must be 1 and 3, in some order.

(They do indeed have a quotient of 3, as shown.) The 3 can't go in the fifth row, because this row already has a 3. So it must go in the fourth row, with the 1 going immediately below it.

Continuing in this way, using these and other techniques left for you to discover, you can work your way around the grid, filling in the rest of the squares. The complete solution is shown here.

12× 3	4	1 1	2÷ 2	20× 5
2 2	15× 3	5	1	4
5× 5	2÷ 1	3 3	20× 4	2 2
1	2	2÷ 4	5	3÷ 3
20× 4	5	2	3 3	1

Volume 2 (Multiplication and Division Only) Notes

- In more advanced KenKen puzzles, cages can have more than two squares. It's okay to repeat a digit within a cage, as long as the digit is not repeated in a row or column.
- Sections with more than two squares will always involve multiplication. Division occurs only in sections with exactly two squares.
- Remember, in doing KenKen, you never have to guess. Every puzzle can be solved by using step-by-step logic. Keep going, and soon you'll be a KenKen master!

Kids can KENKEN™ too!

Will Shortz Presents the Logic Puzzles That Make Math Fun!

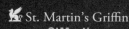

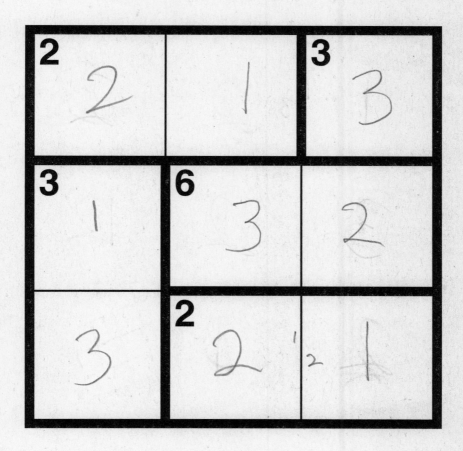

× **1**

2 2	1	**3** 3
3 1	**6** 3	2
3	**2** 2	1

3 — 1	₃ 3	2 — 2
6 — 3	2 — 2	1
2	3 — 1	3

× **3**

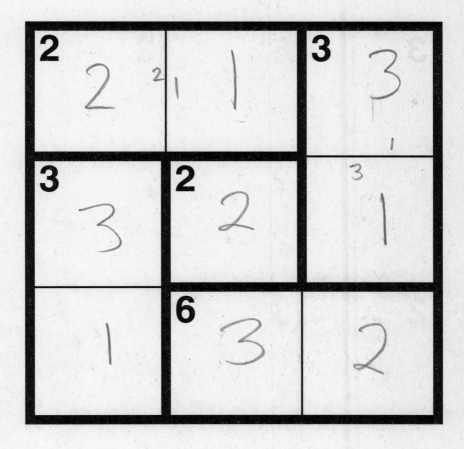

2 2 ²1	1	**3** 3 ₁
3 3	**2** 2	³ 1
1	**6** 3	2

4 ×

3	6	3
1	2	3
3	1	**2** 2
2 2	3	1

$\times$ **5**

2 2	**6** 3	1
3 3	¹3 1	2
2 1	²1 2	**3** 3

6 ×

3 3	1	**12** 2
1	2	3
6 2	3	1

2÷ 1	2	3 3
6× 3	2× 1 ¹2	2
² 2 ³	3× 3	1

8 ×/÷

3× 3	**6×** 2	**1** 1
1	3	**6×** 2
2÷ 2	1	3

×/÷ **9**

3× 3	1	**12×** 2
1	2	3
6× 2	3	1

2 **2**	12 **3**	⁴₃ **4**	3 **1**
4 **4**	1 **1**	6 **2**	**3**
1	8 **2**	**3**	4 **4**
3 **3**	**4**	2 **1**	**2**

× **11**

1 1	**12** 3	4	**2** 2
12 4	**2** 2	**6** 3	1
3	**4** 1	2	**12** 4
2 2	4	**1** 1	3

12 ×

3 3	**2** 2	**4** 1	4
2 2	1	**4** 4	**6** 3 ₂
1	**4** 4	**6** 3 ₂	₃ 2
12 4	3	2 ₃	**1** 1

× **13**

4 4	**2** 2	**2** 1	**3** 3
1	**12** 3	2	**4** 4
6 2	4	**3** 3	1
3	**4** 1	4	**2** 2

14 ×

3 1	3	**4** 4	**8** 2
3 3	**4** 1	**2** 2	4
8 2	4	1	**3** 3
4	**2** 2	**3** 3	1

× **15**

1 1	3 3	8 4	2
6 3	1	2 2 2	12 4 4
2	4 4	1 1	3 3 3
8 4	2	3 3	1

16 ×

8 **2**	12 **3** 4₃ **4**		1 **1**
4	4 **1**	6 **2**	**3**
3 **3** ₃	**4**	1 **1**	8 **2**
1¹	6 **2** ³₂ **3**		**4**

× **17**

6 3	**4** 1 ¹ ₄ 4		**2** 2
2	**12** 4 ₃	**3** 3	1
1 1	⁴ 3	**2** 2	**12** 4 ₃
8 4	2	1	⁴ 3

6 3	**8** 2	4	**4** 1
2	**4** 1	**3** 3	4
4 1	4	**6** 2	3
4	**3** 3	**2** 1	2 1 2

24 4	2	3	**6** 1
2 1	**3** 3	**4** 4	2 $_3$
2	**4** 4	1	3 ^{2}
3 3	1	**8** 2	4

$\times$ **21**

4	2	12	6
4	1	3	2
2 1	2	4	**3**
2	**3** 3	1	**4** 4
24 3	4	2	1

22 ×

6 2 ³2 3		**1** 1	**12** 4
1	**2** 2	**12** 4	⁴ ³3
4 4	1	3	**4** 2
12 3 ⁴3 4		2	1

2 2	1	**12** 4 ^{3}4	3
1	**4** 4	**6** 3 ^{3}2	2
24 4	**6** 3 ^{2} $_3$ 2		**1** 1
3	2	**4** 1	4

24 ×

1 1	**4** 4	**18** 3	2
24 2	1	**4** 4	3
4	**6** 3	2	**4** 1
3	**2** 2	1	4

12 3 ⁴3 4		**4** 1	**2** 2
6 2	3	4	1
4 1	**2** 2	**12** 3	4
4	1	**6** 2	3

12 3 ₃	**4** 1 ⁴¹ 4		**6** 2
⁴ 4	**6** 2 ₃	**2** 1	₃ ² 3
2 1 ₂	² 3	2	**4** 4
2 ¹	**12** 4 ⁴₃ 3		⁴ ¹ 1

× **27**

6 2	3	**4** 4	1
4 4	1	**6** 2	**12** 3
3 1	**8** 2	3	4
3	4	**2** 1	2

28 ×

4 1 ⁴	**12** 4 ⁴ ₃ 3		**2** 2 ₂
¹ 4	**6** 3 ³ ₂ 2		¹ 1
2 2 ₂ ₁ 1		**4** 4 ₁	**12** 3 ⁴
6 3 ² ₃ 2		⁴ 1	³ 4

8 2	**12** 1	4	3
4	**12** 3	**6** 2	**8** 1
3 1	4	3	2
3	**2** 2	1	4

30 ×

6		4	
2 ³₂	3	4 ⁴'₁	1
12 3 ₄	**4** 4 ¹⁴	1	**6** 2 ₃
³ 4	**2** 1 ¹₂	2	² B
1	**24** 2	3	4

× **31**

6			4	
6 3	2	1	**4** 4 ₄	
12 4 ₄ ₃	3	**12** 2	**1** 1	
2 1 ₂	**4** 4 ₁	3	2	
2	₄ 1	**12** 4	3	

32 ×

9 3	**2** 1 ²·¹ 2		**32** 4
1	3	4	2
8 4 ⁴	**6** 2 ²·³ 3		**3** 1
2 ²	**4** 4 ¹·⁴ 1		3

× **33**

12 4	**6** 3 ^{3} $_2$ 2		1
1	**12** 4	3	**24** 2
3	**4** 2	**4** 1	4
2	1	4	3

34 ×

6 2	**12** 1	4 ⁴³	3
3	**8** 2 ⁴	**4** 1 ¹⁴	4
1	4 ²	**6** 3 ²³	2
24 4	3	2	1

× **35**

6 3	**8** 2	1	4
2	**36** 3	4	**12** 1
4 1	**4** 4	3	2
4	4	2	3

?

36 ×

12 1	**12** 4 4/3 3	3	**2** 2 1
4	**12** 3	2	2 1
3	2	**48** 1	4
2 2 2/1	1	4	3

× **37**

2 1	12 4 ⁴ ₃ 3	6 2 ₃
2	8 1	4	² 3
72 4	3	2	4 1
3	2	1	4

2 36
2
18
2
3
3

38 ×/÷

2÷		12×	1
2	4	3 ₄	1
12× 3	**1** 1	4 ³	**6×** 2 ³
4	**2÷** 2	1	3 ²
1 1	**6×** 3 ³	₂ 2	**4** 4

1 1	**12×** 4	**6×** 3 ³₂	2
2÷ 4 ⁴	3	**2÷** 2	1
2 ²	**2÷** 1 ₂	**4** 4	**12×** 3
3 3	2¹	1	4

40 ×/÷

3 3	**16×** 1	4	**2÷** 2
2÷ 2	4	**3** 3	1
1	**6×** 3	2	**12×** 4
8× 4	2	1	3

×/÷ **41**

12× 3	2÷ 2	11	2÷ 4
1	12× 4 4 3	3	2
4	3 3	2÷ 2	1
2÷ 2	1	12× 4 4 3	3

42 ×/÷

2÷ 1	**24×** 2	3	4
2	**12×** 3	**4×** 4	1
12× 3	4	1	**6×** 2
4	**2÷** 1	2	3

×/÷ **43**

2÷ 1 1	**2÷** 4	2	**12×** 3
2	**2÷** 1 2	**12×** 3	4
36× 3	2	4	**2÷** 1
4	3	1	2

44 ×/÷

8× 2 ⁴2 4		**12×** 1	3
3× 1	3	4	**8×** 2
12× 3 ₃	1	**12×** 2	4
⁴4	2	3	1

2÷ 2 ₂ ₁	1	**12×** 4 ⁴ ₃	3
12× 1	**12×** 4 ³ ₄	3	**8×** 2
3	**6×** 2	1	4
4	3	**2÷** 2	1

46 ×/÷

12×		24×	
4	1	3	2
6× 2	3	**2×** 1	4
3	**2÷** 4	2	1
1	2	**12×** 4	3

6×	2÷		48×
3	2	1	4
2	1	4	3
12× 4	3	**2÷** 2	1
1	**24×** 4	3	2

48 ×/÷

2÷ 1	48× 4	3	6× 2
2	6× 1	4	3
24× 4	3	2	4× 1
3	2	1	4

8× 4	1	2	12× 3
12× 2	3	12× 4	1
12× 1	2	3	4
3	4	2÷ 1	2

50 ×/÷

2÷ 1	**2÷** 4	²4 2	**12×** 3
²1 2	**12×** 1	3	4
72× 3	2	4	1
4	3	**2÷** 1	¹2 2

2 36
2 18
2 9
3
3

×/÷ **51**

2×		24×	
2	1	4	3
1	24× 4	3	2
36× 3	2 ²₁	1	8× 4
4	3	2 ²₁	1

```
    36           2 12
  2 18           2 6
   2 9           2 3
    3
    3
```

52 ×/÷

A 4×4 KenKen (×/÷) puzzle grid with handwritten solution:

2÷		48×	
1	2	4	3
6×	24×		
2	3	1	4
			2÷
3	4	2	1
12×			
4	1	3	2

×/÷ **53**

12× 1	3	4	8× 2
12× 3	2÷ 1	2	4
4	16× 2	9× 3	1
2	4	1	3

4342

54 ×/÷

8× 1	4	**6×** 2	3
6× 3	2	**96×** 4	1
2	1	3	4
12× 4	3	1	2

× **55**

1 1	**15×** 5	3	**8×** 4	2
15× 3	**8×** 2	**10×** 5	1	**12×** 4
5	4	2	**15×** 3	1
8× 2	1	4	5	3
12× 4	3	**10×** 1	2	5

951

56 ×

10× 5	1	20× 4	6× 3	2
6× 1	2		20× 5 4	60× 3 4
2	12× 3 3			
3	4 4	4× 2	1	5
60× 4	5	3	2²	1

32×		**30×**		
		15×		**12×**
90×	**40×**			
	40×			

58 ×

300×				30×
	12×		32×	
6×	1200×			

× **59**

1200×			6×	
			20×	48×
10×	24×			
		15×		

60 ×/÷

6×		**1**	**20×**	
20×	**1**	**12×**		**2÷**
	15×		**2÷**	
12×		**2**		**15×**
1	**10×**		**4**	

×/÷ **61**

12×		10×		1
1	20×		2÷	6×
20×		3		
3	2÷		4	20×
2÷		15×		

62 ×/÷

2	60×	10×	1	12×
15×	2÷	20×		15×
		2÷		
	1	24×		

60×			2÷	
1	2÷	15×		12×
40×		2÷		
	15×	12×		10×
			1	

64 ×/÷

40×			12×	
2÷	12×	10×		
			15×	
60×	15×			2÷
		2÷		

15×			80×	6×
2÷				
2÷	15×	20×		
		4×	15×	
12×				

66 ×/÷

2÷		15×		
6×	2÷		75×	2÷
	20×			
			12×	
15×		2÷		

×/÷ **67**

15×	20×		2÷	
		2÷	36×	
20×				2÷
2÷		15×		
6×		20×		

68 ×/÷

80×		2÷	15×	
				2÷
15×		45×	2÷	
2÷				15×
	2÷			

×/÷ **69**

15×	2÷		3×	
	20×	2÷		60×
2÷				
	6×			40×
15×				

6×	2÷		100×	12×
20×	12×		2÷	
	15×	2÷		30×

12×	15×	2÷		2÷
		75×		
10×			2÷	
		4×		45×
2÷				

72 ×/÷

18×		**100×**		**2÷**
20×		**15×**		
			2÷	**12×**
	2÷			
2÷		**60×**		

12×			40×	
15×	30×			2÷
		15×		
	8×	2÷		15×

74 ×/÷

15×	10×			2÷
		12×		
2÷		60×		15×
80×			2÷	
	6×			

2÷		15×		
15×		24×	2÷	
			40×	15×
20×				
	2÷		12×	

76 ×/÷

60×			15×	2÷
2÷	10×			
		2÷	12×	
3×			2÷	15×
	20×			

15×	12×		10×	
	6×			2÷
	2÷	20×		
2÷			15×	
	60×			

78 ×/÷

15×		2÷		12×
2÷		15×		
20×	40×			2÷
	9×		40×	

×/÷ **79**

75×		8×		
	2÷	3×	60×	
2÷				
	12×	10×		2÷
		15×		

80 ×/÷

15×			2÷	
40×	20×			30×
	12×	2÷		
			12×	
30×				

×/÷ **81**

75×		12×	2÷	
6×				60×
	20×		2÷	
	2÷			
2÷		15×		

82 ×/÷

2÷		15×	2÷	30×
60×				
12×				
	30×			20×
	2÷			

2÷		60×		12×
30×	2÷			
		15×		
60×			2÷	
		10×		

84 ×/÷

10×	15×		12×	20×
	2÷			
	9×	2÷		
		100×		6×
2÷				

6×	5	2×	12×	
	4×		15×	4
1		15×		10×
2÷			1	
15×		4	2÷	

86 ×/÷

8×		3	4÷	15×
5	6×	2÷		
4×			5	2÷
	5÷		6×	
15×		4		1

8×		1	15×	
3	4÷	10×		8×
2÷		3	5×	
	5	2÷		3÷
15×			4	

88 ×/÷

2	15×	4÷		3
5×		8×		2÷
	4	3÷	5	
8×			15×	
3×		5	2÷	

6×	15×		1	20×
	1	2÷		
4×	8×		15×	
	6×	5	3÷	
5		4÷		2

90 ×/÷

6×	2÷	20×		3
		15×	1	2÷
4×	5		8×	
	3÷			5
5	8×		3×	

20×	12×	5×		2
		1	6×	
2÷	10×		12×	4
	2÷	3		5÷
3		20×		

92 ×/÷

5	4÷		15×	2÷
6×		1		
3÷	2÷	20×		3
		2	2×	5÷
4	15×			

2÷		2÷	5	24×
15×			4×	
3÷	5÷			
	20×	12×	10×	
2			3÷	

94 ×/÷

2	5×	12×		
12×		10×		20×
	6×		2÷	
5	12×			
4÷		15×		2

×/÷ **95**

4	6×			15×
10×	4÷		20×	
	15×			2
	2÷	10×	3÷	
3			4÷	

96 ×/÷

3	20×			2÷
20×	2÷	3	5×	
		40×		15×
3×			6×	
2÷				1

12×			40×	
2	15×			
20×	2÷		15×	
	6×	4÷		2÷
		15×		

98 ×/÷

2×		60×		
	10×	15×	2÷	
3			20×	2÷
80×	3÷			
		6×		

12×		10×		
	100×	4	18×	2÷
6×		5÷	20×	12×
2÷				

100 ×/÷

2÷	15×	4÷		10×
		6×		
3÷	24×	5		
			240×	
10×				

ANSWERS

1

2 **2**	**1**	3 **3**
3 **1**	6 **3**	**2**
3	2 **2**	**1**

2

3 **1**	**3**	2 **2**
6 **3**	2 **2**	**1**
2	3 **1**	**3**

3

2 **2**	**1**	3 **3**
3 **3**	2 **2**	**1**
1	6 **3**	**2**

4

3 **1**	6 **2**	3 **3**
3	**1**	2 **2**
2 **2**	**3**	**1**

5

2 **2**	6 **3**	**1**
3 **3**	**1**	**2**
2 **1**	**2**	3 **3**

6

3 **3**	**1**	12 **2**
1	**2**	**3**
6 **2**	**3**	**1**

2÷ 1	2	3 3
6× 3	2× 1	2
2	3× 3	1

3× 3	6× 2	1 1
1	3	6× 2
2÷ 2	1	3

3× 3	1	12× 2
1	2	3
6× 2	3	1

2 2	12 3	4	3 1
4 4	1 1	6 2	3
1	8 2	3	4 4
3 3	4	2 1	2

1 1	12 3	4	2 2
12 4	2 2	6 3	1
3	4 1	2	12 4
2 2	4	1 1	3

3 3	2 2	4 1	4
2 2	1	4 4	6 3
1	4 4	6 3	2
12 4	3	2	1 1

13

4^{4}	2^{2}	1^{2}	3^{3}
1	3^{12}	2	4^{4}
2^{6}	4	3^{3}	1
3	1^{4}	4	2^{2}

14

1^{3}	3	4^{4}	2^{8}
3^{3}	1^{4}	2^{2}	4
2^{8}	4	1	3^{3}
4	2^{2}	3^{3}	1

15

1^{1}	3^{3}	4^{8}	2
3^{6}	1	2^{2}	4^{12}
2	4^{4}	1	3
4^{8}	2	3^{3}	1

16

2^{8}	3^{12}	4	1^{1}
4	1^{4}	2^{6}	3
3^{3}	4	1^{1}	2^{8}
1	2^{6}	3	4

17

2^{8}	4^{4}	3^{3}	1
4	2^{2}	1^{4}	3^{6}
3^{3}	1	4	2
1	3^{6}	2	4^{4}

18

3^{6}	1^{4}	4	2^{2}
2	4^{12}	3^{3}	1
1^{1}	3	2^{2}	4^{12}
4^{8}	2	1	3

19

⁶3	⁸2	4	⁴1
2	⁴1	³3	4
⁴1	4	⁶2	3
4	³3	²1	2

20

²⁴4	2	3	⁶1
²1	³3	⁴4	2
2	⁴4	1	3
³3	1	⁸2	4

21

⁴4	²1	¹²3	⁶2
²1	2	4	3
2	³3	1	⁴4
²⁴3	4	2	1

22

⁶2	3	¹1	¹²4
1	²2	¹²4	3
⁴4	1	3	⁴2
¹²3	4	2	1

23

²2	1	¹²4	3
1	⁴4	⁶3	2
²⁴4	⁶3	2	¹1
3	2	⁴1	4

24

¹1	⁴4	¹⁸3	2
²⁴2	1	⁴4	3
4	⁶3	2	⁴1
3	²2	1	4

¹²3	4	⁴1	²2
⁶2	3	4	1
⁴1	²2	¹²3	4
4	1	⁶2	3

¹²3	⁴1	4	⁶2
4	⁶2	²1	3
²1	3	2	⁴4
2	¹²4	3	1

⁶2	3	⁴4	1
⁴4	1	⁶2	¹²3
³1	⁸2	3	4
3	4	²1	2

⁴1	¹²4	3	²2
4	⁶3	2	1
²2	1	⁴4	¹²3
⁶3	2	1	4

⁸2	¹²1	4	3
4	¹²3	⁶2	⁸1
³1	4	3	2
3	²2	1	4

⁶2	3	⁴4	1
¹²3	⁴4	1	⁶2
4	²1	2	3
1	²⁴2	3	4

6 3	2	1	4 4
12 4	3	12 2	1
2 1	4 4	3	2
2	1	12 4	3

9 3	2 1	2	32 4
1	3	4	2
8 4	6 2	3	3 1
2	4 4	1	3

12 4	6 3	2	1
1	12 4	3	24 2
3	4 2	4 1	4
2	1	4	3

6 2	12 1	4	3
3	8 2	4 1	4
1	4	6 3	2
24 4	3	2	1

6 3	8 4	1	2
2	36 3	4	12 1
4 1	4 2	3	4
4	1	2	3

12 1	12 4	3	2 2
4	12 3	2	1
3	2	48 1	4
2 2	1	4	3

² 1	¹² 4	3	⁶ 2
2	⁸ 1	4	3
⁷² 4	3	2	⁴ 1
3	2	1	4

²÷ 2	4	¹²× 3	¹ 1
¹²× 3	¹ 1	4	⁶× 2
4	²÷ 2	1	3
¹ 1	⁶× 3	2	⁴ 4

¹ 1	¹²× 4	⁶× 3	2
²÷ 4	3	²÷ 2	1
2	²÷ 1	⁴ 4	¹²× 3
³ 3	2	1	4

³ 3	¹⁶× 1	4	²÷ 2
²÷ 2	4	³ 3	1
1	⁶× 3	2	¹²× 4
⁸× 4	2	1	3

¹²× 3	²÷ 2	1	²÷ 4
1	¹²× 4	3	2
4	³ 3	²÷ 2	1
²÷ 2	1	¹²× 4	3

²÷ 1	²⁴× 2	3	4
2	¹²× 3	⁴× 4	1
¹²× 3	4	1	⁶× 2
4	²÷ 1	2	3

43

2÷ **1**	2÷ **4**	**2**	12× **3**
2	2÷ **1**	12× **3**	**4**
36× **3**	**2**	**4**	2÷ **1**
4	**3**	**1**	**2**

44

8× **2**	**4**	12× **1**	**3**
3× **1**	**3**	**4**	8× **2**
12× **3**	**1**	12× **2**	**4**
4	**2**	**3**	**1**

45

2÷ **2**	**1**	12× **4**	**3**
12× **1**	12× **4**	**3**	8× **2**
3	6× **2**	**1**	**4**
4	**3**	2÷ **2**	**1**

46

12× **4**	**1**	24× **3**	**2**
6× **2**	**3**	2× **1**	**4**
3	2÷ **4**	**2**	**1**
1	**2**	12× **4**	**3**

47

6× **3**	2÷ **2**	**1**	48× **4**
2	**1**	**4**	**3**
12× **4**	**3**	2÷ **2**	**1**
1	24× **4**	**3**	**2**

48

2÷ **1**	48× **4**	**3**	6× **2**
2	6× **1**	**4**	**3**
24× **4**	**3**	**2**	4× **1**
3	**2**	**1**	**4**

49

8× 4	1	2	12× 3
12× 2	3	12× 4	1
12× 1	2	3	4
3	4	2÷ 1	2

50

2÷ 1	2÷ 4	2	12× 3
2	12× 1	3	4
72× 3	2	4	1
4	3	2÷ 1	2

51

2× 2	1	24× 4	3
1	24× 4	3	2
36× 3	2	1	8× 4
4	3	2	1

52

2÷ 1	2	48× 4	3
6× 2	24× 3	1	4
3	4	2	2÷ 1
12× 4	1	3	2

53

12× 1	3	4	8× 2
12× 3	2÷ 1	2	4
4	16× 2	9× 3	1
2	4	1	3

54

8× 1	4	6× 2	3
6× 3	2	96× 4	1
2	1	3	4
12× 4	3	1	2

55

¹1	¹⁵ˣ5	3	⁸ˣ4	2
¹⁵ˣ3	⁸ˣ2	¹⁰ˣ5	1	¹²ˣ4
5	4	2	¹⁵ˣ3	1
⁸ˣ2	1	4	5	3
¹²ˣ4	3	¹⁰ˣ1	2	5

56

¹⁰ˣ5	1	²⁰ˣ4	⁶ˣ3	2
⁶ˣ1	2	5	²⁰ˣ4	⁶⁰ˣ3
2	¹²ˣ3	1	5	4
3	4	⁴ˣ2	1	5
⁶⁰ˣ4	5	3	2	1

57

³²ˣ1	4	³⁰ˣ3	2	5
4	2	¹⁵ˣ1	5	¹²ˣ3
⁹⁰ˣ2	⁴⁰ˣ5	4	3	1
5	3	2	1	4
3	⁴⁰ˣ1	5	4	2

58

³⁰⁰ˣ4	5	1	3	³⁰ˣ2
5	¹²ˣ1	2	³²ˣ4	3
2	3	4	1	5
⁶ˣ3	¹²⁰⁰ˣ4	5	2	1
1	2	3	5	4

59

¹²⁰⁰ˣ4	1	5	⁶ˣ3	2
3	5	4	²⁰ˣ2	⁴⁸ˣ1
¹⁰ˣ1	²⁴ˣ3	2	5	4
5	2	1	4	3
2	4	¹⁵ˣ3	1	5

60

⁶ˣ2	3	¹1	²⁰ˣ5	4
²⁰ˣ5	¹1	¹²ˣ4	3	²÷2
4	¹⁵ˣ5	3	²÷2	1
¹²ˣ3	4	²2	1	¹⁵ˣ5
¹1	¹⁰ˣ2	5	⁴4	3

61

12× 4	3	10× 2	5	1× 1
1× 1	20× 5	4	2÷ 2	6× 3
20× 5	4	3× 3	1	2
3× 3	2÷ 2	1	4× 4	20× 5
2÷ 2	1	15× 5	3	4

62

2× 2	60× 3	10× 5	1× 1	12× 4
4	5	2	3	1
15× 1	2÷ 2	20× 4	5	15× 3
3	4	2÷ 1	2	5
5	1× 1	24× 3	4	2

63

60× 3	4	5	2÷ 2	1
1× 1	2÷ 2	15× 3	5	12× 4
40× 5	1	2÷ 2	4	3
4	15× 5	12× 1	3	10× 2
2	3	4	1× 1	5

64

40× 5	2	4	12× 1	3
2÷ 1	12× 3	10× 5	2	4
2	4	1	15× 3	5
60× 4	15× 1	3	5	2÷ 2
3	5	2÷ 2	4	1

65

15× 5	1	3	80× 4	6× 2
2÷ 1	2	4	5	3
2÷ 2	15× 3	20× 5	1	4
4	5	4× 2	15× 3	1
12× 3	4	1	2	5

66

2÷ 4	2	15× 3	1	5
6× 3	2÷ 1	2	75× 5	2÷ 4
1	20× 4	5	3	2
2	5	1	12× 4	3
15× 5	3	2÷ 4	2	1

67

15× 3	20× 4	5	2÷ 2	1
5	1	2÷ 2	36× 4	3
20× 4	5	1	3	2÷ 2
2÷ 1	2	15× 3	5	4
6× 2	3	20× 4	1	5

68

80× 4	5	2÷ 2	15× 1	3
15× 3	4	1	5	2÷ 2
5	1	45× 3	2÷ 2	4
2÷ 2	3	5	4	15× 1
1	2÷ 2	4	3	5

69

15× 5	2÷ 2	4	3× 3	1
3	20× 5	2÷ 2	1	60× 4
2÷ 2	4	1	5	3
4	6× 1	3	2	40× 5
15× 1	3	5	4	2

70

6× 3	2÷ 2	1	100× 5	12× 4
2	1	5	4	3
20× 5	12× 4	3	2÷ 2	1
4	15× 3	2÷ 2	1	30× 5
1	5	4	3	2

71

12× 3	15× 5	2÷ 2	4	2÷ 1
4	1	75× 3	5	2
10× 1	3	5	2÷ 2	4
5	2	4× 4	1	45× 3
2÷ 2	4	1	3	5

72

18× 3	2	100× 5	4	2÷ 1
20× 4	3	15× 1	5	2
1	5	3	2÷ 2	12× 4
5	2÷ 4	2	1	3
2÷ 2	1	60× 4	3	5

73

12× 4	3	1	40× 2	5
15× 1	30× 5	3	4	2÷ 2
3	2	15× 5	1	4
5	8× 4	2÷ 2	3	15× 1
2	1	4	5	3

74

15× 3	10× 2	1	5	2÷ 4
1	5	12× 4	3	2
2÷ 2	1	60× 5	4	15× 3
80× 5	4	3	2÷ 2	1
4	6× 3	2	1	5

75

2÷ 2	4	15× 3	5	1
15× 3	5	24× 4	2÷ 1	2
1	3	2	40× 4	15× 5
20× 4	1	5	2	3
5	2÷ 2	1	12× 3	4

76

60× 5	3	4	15× 1	2÷ 2
2÷ 4	10× 2	3	5	1
2	5	2÷ 1	12× 3	4
3× 3	1	2	2÷ 4	15× 5
1	20× 4	5	2	3

77

15× 1	12× 4	3	10× 2	5
5	6× 3	2	1	2÷ 4
3	2÷ 1	20× 5	4	2
2÷ 4	2	1	15× 5	3
2	60× 5	4	3	1

78

15× 3	5	2÷ 2	1	12× 4
2÷ 2	4	15× 1	5	3
20× 5	40× 2	4	3	2÷ 1
1	9× 3	5	40× 4	2
4	1	3	2	5

79

3 (75×)	**5**	**4** (8×)	**2**	**1**
5	**2** (2÷)	**1** (3×)	**4** (60×)	**3**
2 (2÷)	**4**	**3**	**1**	**5**
1	**3** (12×)	**2** (10×)	**5**	**4** (2÷)
4	**1**	**5** (15×)	**3**	**2**

80

1 (15×)	**5**	**3**	**4** (2÷)	**2**
2 (40×)	**1** (20×)	**4**	**5**	**3** (30×)
4	**3** (12×)	**1** (2÷)	**2**	**5**
5	**4**	**2**	**3** (12×)	**1**
3 (30×)	**2**	**5**	**1**	**4**

81

5 (75×)	**3**	**4** (12×)	**1** (2÷)	**2**
2 (6×)	**5**	**1**	**3**	**4** (60×)
1	**4** (20×)	**5**	**2** (2÷)	**3**
3	**1** (2÷)	**2**	**4**	**5**
4 (2÷)	**2**	**3** (15×)	**5**	**1**

82

2 (2÷)	**1**	**3** (15×)	**4** (2÷)	**5** (30×)
5 (60×)	**4**	**1**	**2**	**3**
4 (12×)	**3**	**5**	**1**	**2**
1	**5** (30×)	**2**	**3**	**4** (20×)
3	**2** (2÷)	**4**	**5**	**1**

83

2 (2÷)	**1**	**4** (60×)	**5**	**3** (12×)
5 (30×)	**4** (2÷)	**2**	**3**	**1**
3	**2**	**5** (15×)	**1**	**4**
1 (60×)	**5**	**3**	**4** (2÷)	**2**
4	**3**	**1** (10×)	**2**	**5**

84

2 (10×)	**5** (15×)	**3**	**4** (12×)	**1** (20×)
1	**4** (2÷)	**2**	**3**	**5**
5	**3** (9×)	**1** (2÷)	**2**	**4**
3	**1**	**4** (100×)	**5**	**2** (6×)
4 (2÷)	**2**	**5**	**1**	**3**

85

6× 2	5	2× 1	12× 4	3
3	4× 1	2	15× 5	4
1	4	15× 5	3	10× 2
2÷ 4	2	3	1	5
15× 5	3	4	2÷ 2	1

86

8× 2	4	3	4÷ 1	15× 5
5	6× 2	2÷ 1	4	3
4× 1	3	2	5	2÷ 4
4	5÷ 1	5	6× 3	2
15× 3	5	4	2	1

87

8× 4	2	1	15× 3	5
3	4÷ 1	10× 5	2	8× 4
2÷ 1	4	3	5× 5	2
2	5	2÷ 4	1	3÷ 3
15× 5	3	2	4	1

88

2	15× 5	4÷ 4	1	3
5× 5	3	8× 2	4	2÷ 1
1	4	3÷ 3	5	2
8× 4	2	1	15× 3	5
3× 3	1	5	2÷ 2	4

89

6× 2	15× 5	3	1	20× 4
3	1	2÷ 4	2	5
4× 1	8× 4	2	15× 5	3
4	6× 2	5	3÷ 3	1
5	3	4÷ 1	4	2

90

6× 2	2÷ 1	20× 4	5	3
3	2	15× 5	1	2÷ 4
4× 1	5	3	8× 4	2
4	3÷ 3	1	2	5
5	8× 4	2	3× 3	1

91

20× 4	12× 3	5× 5	1	2· 2
5	4	¹ 1	6× 2	3
2÷ 1	10× 5	2	12× 3	⁴ 4
2	2÷ 1	³ 3	4	5÷ 5
³ 3	2	20× 4	5	1

92

⁵ 5	4÷ 1	4	15× 3	2÷ 2
6× 2	3	¹ 1	5	4
3÷ 1	2÷ 2	20× 5	4	³ 3
3	4	² 2	2× 1	5÷ 5
⁴ 4	15× 5	3	2	1

93

2÷ 4	2	2÷ 1	⁵ 5	24× 3
15× 5	3	2	4× 1	4
3÷ 3	5÷ 1	5	4	2
1	20× 4	12× 3	10× 2	5
² 2	5	4	3÷ 3	1

94

² 2	5× 5	12× 1	4	3
12× 3	1	10× 2	5	20× 4
4	6× 2	3	2÷ 1	5
⁵ 5	12× 3	4	2	1
4÷ 1	4	15× 5	3	² 2

95

⁴ 4	6× 3	1	2	15× 5
10× 2	4÷ 1	4	20× 5	3
1	15× 5	3	4	² 2
5	2÷ 4	10× 2	3÷ 3	1
³ 3	2	5	4÷ 1	4

96

³ 3	20× 5	1	4	2÷ 2
20× 5	2÷ 2	³ 3	5× 1	4
4	1	40× 2	5	15× 3
3× 1	3	4	6× 2	5
2÷ 2	4	5	3	¹ 1

12× 3	1	4	40× 2	5
2 2	15× 5	3	1	4
20× 1	2÷ 4	2	15× 5	3
5	6× 3	4÷ 1	4	2÷ 2
4	2	15× 5	3	1

2× 2	1	60× 4	3	5
1	10× 5	15× 3	2÷ 2	4
3 3	2	5	20× 4	2÷ 1
80× 4	3÷ 3	1	5	2
5	4	6× 2	1	3

12× 4	3	10× 2	1	5
1	100× 5	4 4	18× 3	2÷ 2
5	4	3	2	1
6× 3	2	5÷ 1	20× 5	12× 4
2÷ 2	1	5	4	3

2÷ 2	15× 3	4÷ 4	1	10× 5
4	5	6× 1	3	2
3÷ 3	24× 4	5 5	2	1
1	2	3	240× 5	4
10× 5	1	2	4	3